COAL

COAL

BY
BETSY HARVEY
KRAFT

FRANKLIN WATTS
NEW YORK I LONDON I TORONTO I SYDNEY I 1982
A FIRST BOOK I REVISED EDITION

45139

Cover photograph courtesy of
the National Coal Association.

Photographs courtesy of Erie Lackawanna Railway:
p. 5; United States Bureau of Mines: p. 8; Federal
Energy Administration: p. 77; National Coal Association: pp. 18, 20, 28, 43, 50; The Nourse Co.: p.
19; Consolidation Coal Co.: pp. 21, 40; B. F. Good-
rich Industrial Products Co.: p. 22; Jeffrey Mining
Machinery Division: p. 23; Joy Manufacturing Co.: p.
14; Bucyrus-Erie Co.: pp. 26, 27; Bethlehem Steel
Corp.: pp. 33, 48; Monterey Coal Co.: p. 41; Ogle-
bay Norton Co.: p. 54; Amax Coal Co.: p. 54; Insti-
tute of Gas Technology: p. 58.

Library of Congress Cataloging in Publication Data

Kraft, Betsy Harvey.
Coal.

(A First book)
Includes index.
Summary: Discusses the history, mining, and uses
of coal, and its effect on the environment, today
and in the future.
1. Coal—Juvenile literature.
[1. Coal] I. Title.
TP325.K643   1982   662.6′2   82-2688
ISBN 0-531-00336-1   AACR2

CONTENTS

COAL

1

COAL THROUGH
THE YEARS

When your grandparents were young, everyone knew what coal looked like. People burned it in their fireplaces and furnaces to heat their homes. The trains they rode in burned coal in their locomotives. Factories burned coal and sent black plumes of smoke billowing into the sky.

Today coal is almost invisible. But it is still very much a part of our lives. When you turn on your television set or the light in your room, chances are more than half that the electricity you are using is generated from coal. The steel in your family's automobile or your city's buses or subway cars was made with **coke**—a product that comes from coal. The concrete used for the sidewalks in your neighborhood was baked in an oven fired with coal. The records you play on your phonograph may very likely have been made from a substance left after coal is burned. When you are sick, your doctor may prescribe a medicine that uses a coal chemical for its base. Farmers use fertilizers made from coal for their crops.

Each year we burn millions of tons of coal. But for centuries it lay buried in the ground unused, because people did not know how to mine it. Occasionally, though, there would be outcroppings of coal at the earth's surface, and curious people who happened upon them discovered that the black rocks would burn.

About three thousand years ago the Chinese began burning coal. Sometimes they used it to heat iron and copper to very high temperatures so that the metals could be bent into useful shapes. Marco Polo, an early Italian explorer who visited China, later wrote about the "black stones" that people dug out of the mountains and burned. The Chinese loved to take baths, Marco Polo noticed. Since there were many people and not enough wood to go around, they used coal instead of wood to heat the water for their tubs.

Ancient Greek blacksmiths also used coal hundreds of years ago to produce the red-hot embers they needed to heat their forges. Historians tell us that when Roman soldiers invaded England, about two thousand years ago, they built their camps near coal outcroppings. They were thus able to use the fuel to keep their fires burning in that chilly northern land.

Many years after the Romans had left, in the early part of the thirteenth century, the English rediscovered coal. In northern England, near the North Sea, there was a large area near the Tyne River where coal was found lying on the earth's surface. The English began to collect this coal and put it to use. They also sent some to France, loading it on ships at Newcastle, a nearby seaport. Coal from this area came to be known as **sea coal**.

In London, the large city to the south, people burned coal in their homes, though it gave off a great deal of smoke and left an unpleasant odor.

In the year 1666 a terrible fire swept through London, destroying houses, shops, and churches. To help rebuild the city, the government placed a tax on all coal that was sent out of the country. The money raised this way helped rebuild many of the city's buildings, including the famous Saint Paul's Cathedral.

The city officials wanted the money to help repair the damage from the fire. But they were also concerned that if much more coal was sent abroad, there would not be enough left to fill the needs at home. They did not realize then that there was enough coal under England's soil to last for hundreds of years.

By the time of the Great Fire of London, brickmakers were burning coal to heat their kilns. In turn, the bricks they made were used to build chimneys for coal-burning fireplaces. Glassblowers used coal too, though the smoke made them ill. Finally they developed ovens where the fumes went up the chimney.

But it was not until the 1700s that England began to mine coal on a large scale. About 1710 a man named Abraham Darby discovered he could bake coal to produce coke—a substance that could be used to make steel from iron ore. Up until this time the steel makers had used charcoal, made from burning wood. Since the forests of England were growing thin, the manufacturers were glad to have this new substitute.

About thirty years after Darby made his discovery, a Scotch inventor named James Watt developed the modern steam engine. Machines were already being used in the textile factories of England. Workers were spinning and weaving with shuttles and looms powered by water. But these water-driven machines had to be located near a stream or river. Watt's engine, on the other hand, was run by steam. It could be brought to wherever it was needed.

The world now had a machine that did not depend on either

water or wind for its power. But it did need fuel. Wherever the steam engine was brought in, the need for fuel went with it. Watt's invention created quite a demand for coal. And, in fact, it was Watt's engine that made it possible to dig coal that had not been mined before.

For years a few brave people had attempted to mine the coal that lay under the earth's surface. But it was dangerous work and water often flooded the pits. The steam engine provided miners with a pump that would keep the floor of the mine dry while they worked.

Watt's engine, then, really marked the beginning of the modern coal industry. By 1854 England was mining almost 65 million tons of coal a year—a far cry from the days when the country's rulers feared that their supply would run out.

Across the Atlantic, in the United States, the coal industry was slower to get under way. Most of the early factories in America were located in the New England states, where water power was plentiful and where there were thick forests that could be cut down and used for fuel.

Early in America's history, about seven hundred years ago, Indians had used coal to fire their pottery. Later, the early explorers Marquette and Joliet had discovered coal on the riverbanks as they made their way across the new land. But they regarded coal more as a curiosity than as a fuel that could provide power for the new nation they were charting.

When the country was more settled, farmers would at times discover coal on their land and dig it from the ground to use on their farms. Sometimes they sold it to neighbors or blacksmiths. They sold it in small amounts, usually by the bushel basketful. Most farmers were not happy about going underground, however. But a few

Coal-burning locomotives, like the one
shown here, were in use by the 1860s.

of them did help out in nearby underground mines during the winter months when there was little for them to do on their farms.

These were small operations, though. It was not until 1750 that the first commercial coal mine opened up near Richmond, Virginia. The coal was dug from the surface and sent to a nearby factory that made ammunition. During the Revolutionary War, it made ammunition for the American soldiers.

But wood was still plentiful in America then. It was not until about a hundred years later that Americans began to need large amounts of coal. By then, steel makers had adopted Darby's use of coke instead of charcoal. Also, by the middle of the 1800s the railroads were becoming popular and coal was needed to run the giant locomotives. And as the rails of the train systems branched outward through the country, a way was provided for coal to be carried from the mine to customers hundreds of miles away. By the year 1900 the railroads alone were using about 75 million tons of coal a year. Homeowners were also using coal in their furnaces and fireplaces.

Once the United States had been a country made up of farmers and tradespeople. Now all that was changing. The railroads, the steel mills, and factories of all kinds were changing the country into an industrial giant. And coal was the fuel that made that change possible.

THE FORMING
OF COAL

When you pick up a lump of coal, it looks black. But if you take a very thin slice of that lump and put it under a powerful microscope, you will see bands of color—yellow, orange, red, and, of course, black. These are the colors of the various elements that make up a lump of coal.

Scientists say that coal was formed about 300 million years ago, in a time known as the **Carboniferous Period** or **Coal Age**. This age lasted about 60 million years. During that time giant plants and trees grew in swamps that covered large portions of the earth, such as the Appalachian region of Pennsylvania. These plants, like plants today, contained the elements oxygen, hydrogen, and carbon. When the plants died, they fell into the water and were covered by layers of sand and mud. As new plants grew, they too died and sank into the water. As more years passed, mud and sand washed over the layers.

PEAT BOG

PEAT

LIGNITE

BITUMINOUS

ANTHRACITE

Types of Coal

The earth was young then and always changing its shape. As the ground shifted above the plant layers, its weight pressed down on the plants. This squeezed out much of the moisture, hydrogen, and oxygen, leaving rich deposits of carbon, the element that allows coal to burn and give off heat. The mud and sand were compressed too, becoming shale, sandstone, and limestone. These are the layers usually found above and below today's coal seams. Sometimes in a seam of coal a miner will find the imprint of one of the ancient plants that went into the making of coal.

During the Coal Age, scientists have observed, some of the plant layers received more pressure than others. The layers receiving the least pressure eventually became a spongy substance known as **peat**. Peat is not really a form of coal. It contains more moisture and less carbon than coal. It can be burned, however, even though it gives off a good deal of smoke and not much heat. In the United States we mix peat with dirt in our gardens to help plants grow better. But in Ireland peat is dug from the ground, dried, and burned in furnaces and electric generation plants.

In those early days when coal was being formed, some layers of peat were pressed down by the earth above and the moisture was squeezed from them, leaving more carbon and producing **lignite**, or brown coal. Lignite, too, was subjected to pressure from the overlying earth. As it became harder and blacker, it formed carbon-rich **sub-bituminous** (very soft) and **bituminous** (soft) coal. (Even though bituminous coal is called soft coal it is really hard and must be broken with a hammer.) **Anthracite**, or what is sometimes called "hard coal," was formed under the greatest pressure of all.

Coal is actually classified now by how much heat it produces when burned. The more carbon-rich the coal is, the more heat it gives off. Thus lignite gives off the least heat, sub-bituminous more, and so on.

Bituminous coal is the most plentiful form of coal we have in the United States. When one pound of bituminous coal is burned, it gives off about 12,000 British Thermal Units of heat, or enough to raise the temperature of 12,000 pounds of water one degree.

Anthracite has more carbon than all other types of coal. It burns easily and produces little smoke and high heat. But there is very little of it to be found in the United States—and most of what is here is located in Pennsylvania.

Lignite has less carbon and more moisture than sub-bituminous or bituminous coal and is found mostly in the western states in America. Until very recently, not much lignite was mined in our country. But because our energy needs are growing, more lignite is now being mined and new ways to use it are being developed.

The United States has over one-fourth of all the recoverable coal in the world, Russia about one-fourth, and China more than one-tenth. Australia, South Africa, Canada, Poland, Germany, France, Britain, and Belgium also have large deposits, or reserves.

If you look at a map of the United States showing where coal is located, you will see that there are three main coal areas. On the East Coast, bituminous coal fields stretch north from Alabama through Kentucky, West Virginia, Virginia, Pennsylvania, and Ohio. You will also see a small area in Pennsylvania showing the location of deposits of anthracite coal.

In the Midwest there is more bituminous coal lying under the ground in Indiana, Illinois, and western Kentucky. Just west of this bed lies a large coal area under Iowa, Missouri, Kansas, Oklahoma, and part of Texas. The western coal beds, made up mostly of lignite

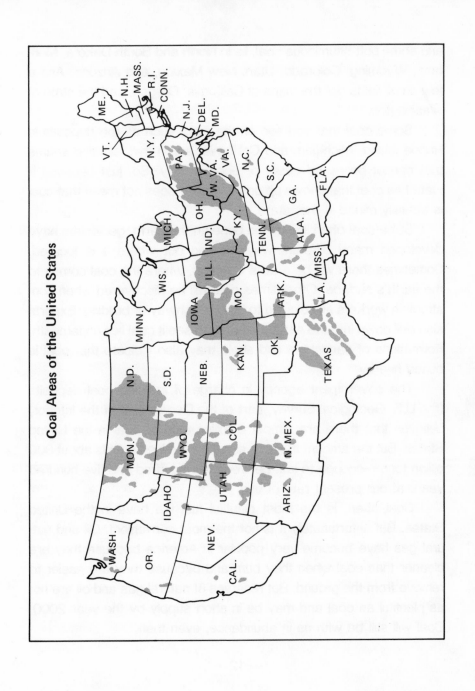

Coal Areas of the United States

and some soft bituminous coal, lie in North and South Dakota, Montana, Wyoming, Colorado, Utah, New Mexico, and Arizona. And a few small fields dot the maps of California, Oregon, and the state of Washington.

Some coal that you see on the map, such as the deposits in Rhode Island, Michigan, and California, are in thin, slanting seams that cannot be mined easily or economically. So, just because a state has coal that shows up on the map, it does not mean that coal is actually mined in that state.

Since coal often lies buried beneath the earth, geologists have developed many different ways to find out where it is located. Sometimes there will be a **coal outcrop**, where the coal comes to the earth's surface. Other times coal will be discovered when construction workers are digging to build a highway or building. Experts also drill down into the earth's surface to see if coal lies underneath. Formations of sandstone and shale may also indicate that coal is buried nearby.

The government agency in charge of locating coal deposits (the U.S. Geological Survey, part of the Department of the Interior) believes that there are almost 4 trillion tons of coal in the United States. But the amount that can actually be mined equals about 300 billion tons—enough to last between two hundred and five hundred years at our present rate of use.

Coal, then, is the most plentiful fuel we have in the United States. But unfortunately it is not the most convenient. Oil and natural gas have become very popular in America because they are cleaner than coal when they burn and because they are easier to remove from the ground. But reserves of natural gas and oil are not as plentiful as coal and may be in short supply by the year 2000. Coal will still be with us in abundance, even then.

HOW COAL
IS MINED

Much of the coal in the United States lies buried deep in the ground. It must be reached by building shafts or tunnels that lead down to the coal seam. These are called **underground mines**. Other coal lies closer to the earth's surface and can be removed by simply using machines to dig away the layer of dirt that covers the seam. This operation is called **surface,** or **strip, mining.**

DEVELOPING THE MINE

A little less than half the coal mined in the United States comes from underground mines. There are three types of underground mines that coal companies build to get at the coal: **shaft, drift,** or **slope mines.** The kind used depends on where the coal lies in relation to the earth's surface.

In a shaft mine a vertical hole is drilled to reach the level of the coal seam. The coal seam may lie hundreds of feet beneath the

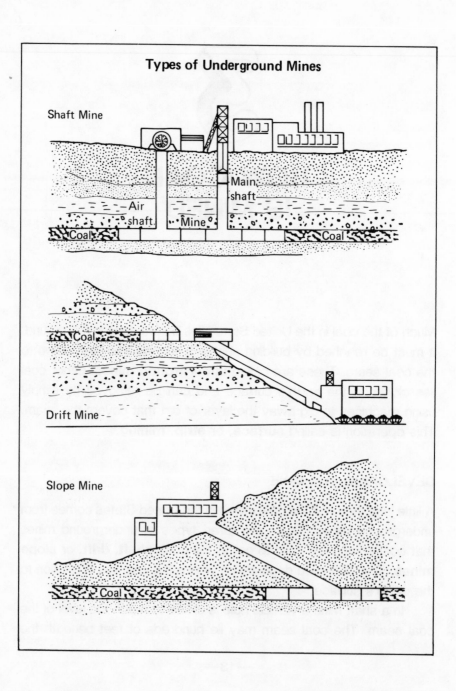

Types of Underground Mines

Shaft Mine

Main shaft

Air shaft

Mine

Coal

Coal

Drift Mine

Coal

Slope Mine

Coal

ground. A large elevator, or *cage*, is constructed to take miners down to the coal seam.

When a coal seam lies fairly close to the surface of the earth, a slope mine will be developed instead. In this case a sloping tunnel is dug out. It reaches from the entrance down through the ground to the coal seam. Miners usually walk through the tunnel to the working area in the mine.

When coal is exposed on the hillside a drift mine is set up. The miners mine the coal as they move along, creating a horizontal tunnel or passageway. As more and more coal is removed, the miners walk farther and farther into the hillside to reach the working area, or **coal face**.

In an underground mine the miners dig tunnels back through the coal seam, leaving large blocks of coal between the tunnels to support the roof. If you looked at a map of a coal mine, it would look like a map of a small city. The tunnels are, in a way, the streets of the mine.

Once the tunnels reach the end of the coal seam, the miners start mining backwards, taking the large blocks of coal left in-between the tunnels, allowing the roof to collapse behind them as they go. This way they work their way back to the entrance of the mine. This entire operation may take ten years or more, depending on how large the coal seam is.

When all the coal has been removed from a mine, the mine is closed. This process usually takes several years. A mine that has been closed is referred to as having been "mined out."

UNDERGROUND MINING

When miners arrive at the level of the coal, they get into electric-powered cars that look like small open-topped railroad cars and ride to the coal face. These *mantrip* cars, as they are known, travel through the tunnels—often several miles—to the sections where coal will be mined that day.

The miners work together in groups, or *section crews*. There may be several different section crews working at one time in various parts of the mine. Each person in the crew performs a specific job in helping to mine the coal.

Before any mining can begin, however, certain safety measures must be taken. One of the miners tests the air in the section to make sure that there are no dangerous gases present. A miner known as a *rock duster* then sprays the walls and ceiling of the work area with powdered limestone. This settles any dust that might cause an explosion. A third miner, called a *roof bolter*, inserts long steel rods into the ceiling area. This prevents roof cave-ins. The steel rods actually hold the overlying layers of rock together. (For more on mine safety, see the chapter "Making Mining Safer.")

About 40 percent of the coal in underground mining is removed by a three-step method called *conventional mining*. First a miner cuts a deep slice of coal, or *kerf*, near the floor of the mine, using a mechanical cutting machine mounted on wheels. Then a *shot firer* drills a number of holes higher up and deep back into the coal face. Special safety-approved explosives or cartridges of compressed air are then placed in the holes. When the explosives are set off, a section of the coal face shatters. The pieces fall into the slot made by the cutting machine. Next a miner operating a *loading machine* moves in. The machine scoops the coal from the mine floor and dumps it into a waiting *shuttle* car. The shuttle car takes the coal to a central dumping spot where the coal is put on a *conveyor belt* that takes it to an elevator, or *skip hoist*, that lifts it out of the mine. (In slope and drift mines the coal travels all the way out of the mine by conveyor belt.)

Beginning their workday, miners board the steel-topped
mantrip cars to ride to the working face of the mine.

To keep down coal dust, a miner sprays powdered limestone over the exposed coal surfaces in a low coal seam. Opposite: miners use a machine to insert roof bolts that help support the ceiling.

A high-speed drill is used to bore holes into the coal face. Explosives or compressed-air cartridges are then placed in the holes and set off to shatter coal for loading.

A loading machine sweeps
the shattered coal onto
its conveyor belt and then
into a shuttle car.

The head of this continuous miner was designed to cut
an arched roof as it rips coal from the seam. Gathering
arms and a conveyor belt pick up the coal and deliver it
to waiting shuttle cars. Opposite: this conveyor belt is
hauling coal from the mine directly to the cleaning plant
above the ground. It can handle 1,800 tons an hour.

A miner moves the hydraulic roof support as this longwall mining machine advances. The cable (left) pulls the shearer across the coal face, and broken coal drops into the conveyor belt below.

More than half of today's underground coal is mined by a giant machine called the *continuous miner*. It is a type of tractor with wheels and large rotating teeth at one end. These teeth are moved into place against the coal face. As the teeth turn, they shear the coal into thousands of small pieces. Another part of the machine scoops up and loads these pieces onto a shuttle car. Again, the shuttle car carries the coal to the mine's conveyor belt.

One person operating a continuous miner can mine up to 12 tons of coal an hour. However, the machines seldom work full time. The miners must stop from time to time to change shuttle cars, retest the air for dangerous gases, insert new roof bolts, and spray the newly exposed areas with powdered limestone.

Finally, a few underground mines in the United States use a machine called a *longwall miner*. In longwalling, a steel blade slices off a long section of the coal face. The sliced-off coal falls onto a conveyor belt located under the blade. It is then carried away from the face. The longwall machine has overhead braces. These braces move ahead to support the roof, so that it will not collapse as the coal is removed.

SURFACE, OR STRIP, MINING

When coal is mined at a surface mine, it can be removed much more quickly and safely than from an underground mine. The miners use large electric shovels or *draglines* to remove the rock and dirt, called **overburden,** that lies above the coal seam. Some of the largest shovels are more than fifty stories high. The *cab,* or small room where the operator sits, is usually air-conditioned and has a large panel of control buttons that the operator uses to direct the machine. These can remove more than 300 tons of overburden in one bite.

This dragline, one of the largest in the world,
weighs 27 million pounds (12.2 million kg). It can
pick up about 325 tons of rock and dirt at one bite.
Opposite: this dipper of a surface coal mining
shovel can move about three railroad carloads of dirt
and rock once every minute. Note how small the man
on the left appears standing beside the dipper.

A view of the pit from
the shovel operator's position

First, the overburden is broken up with explosives. Then the shovel operator directs the machine to pile the overburden on one side. Then the exposed coal is scooped up by smaller mechanical shovels and loaded into giant trucks. When all the coal has been removed from the pit, the miners move the overburden back into the pit. They then move on to another section of the coal seam, where they start the process all over again.

Sometimes coal lies buried in a hillside but is too close to the surface to be underground-mined. This coal is removed by *auger mining*. An auger is a large mechanical bit that looks like a giant carpenter's drill. It bores into a hillside and draws the coal out from the seam, onto a conveyor belt that loads it onto a truck. Augering is usually considered a kind of strip mining.

There are advantages to mining coal on the surface. It is safer, easier, and less expensive. But often productive land is torn up in the process. For years most coal companies left the land they strip-mined unshaped and unplanted. As a result it remained bare and ugly. Now there is a federal law that requires coal companies to reshape the land that they strip-mine, to plant and tend it, and to make sure that it is returned to a useful purpose. Returning the land to a productive state is called reclamation.

In 1980 miners in the United States produced approximately 830 million tons of coal from surface and underground mines—more coal than has ever been produced in this country before. With our population growing, with more and more industry developing, and with gas and oil in shorter supply miners will probably be called upon to mine even more coal in the years to come.

MAKING MINING SAFER

No matter what method is used to remove the coal, safety is a major concern in the mine. For years coal mining was one of the world's most dangerous occupations. But in recent years the mines have become much safer places in which to work. In 1930, 1,619 miners were killed in mining accidents. By 1980 this figure had dropped to 129.

Miners who work underground wear special safety clothing that they put on before they go into the mine. They wear hard hats with electric lamps on them and special steel-toed boots that protect their feet. On their belts they have a special piece of equipment called a *self-rescuer*. This supplies them with good air to breathe in case the air in the mine becomes filled with unhealthy gases. They also have a mask, called a *respirator*, that they wear over their mouth and nose in particularly dusty parts of the mine. At surface mines, miners also wear hard hats and special shoes.

All new miners in the United States must, by law, be trained in safe ways of mining before they can work either at a surface or an underground mine. They also learn first aid. And there are special rescue teams that are trained to go into underground mines in case miners are trapped during an explosion or accident in the mine.

Underground mines can be dangerous mainly because of the deadly gases that often lie hidden deep in coal seams, and because sections of the roof can fall in if the ceiling is not properly supported.

Sometimes a coal seam will contain a gas made up mostly of carbon dioxide and very little oxygen. Healthy air has a high oxygen content. Without enough oxygen in the air, people cannot breathe. Miners used to test for this gas by carrying candles with them into the tunnels. The flame would not burn without a proper supply of oxygen. Thus, if the flame went out, the miners knew that dangerous gases were present. But these open flames were dangerous and sometimes caused explosions. In 1816 an English inventor, Sir Humphry Davy, developed a special safety lamp. The flame of this lamp was enclosed in wire mesh, so that it could not ignite and cause an explosion.

Methane, another gas, is also found in some coal seams. It can, if enough of it mixes with air, cause an explosion. Today miners use an electronic device known as a **methane monitor.** This instrument shows the miners whether or not methane is present in the mine. Because of the possibility of fire or explosion, miners are not allowed to smoke in the mines.

Although explosions do still occur sometimes in underground mines, often killing several miners at one time, most of the fatal accidents occur because of roof falls. In 1980 roof falls accounted for the deaths of 30 miners. Other miners have been killed in accidents relating to hauling coal from the face and from mishandling machinery or electrical equipment.

A hazard that the modern underground miner should no longer have to face is a disease known as **black lung**. Black lung comes from breathing in coal dust for very long periods of time. It causes shortness of breath and, in extreme cases, even death. By federal law the dust levels must now be kept very low in underground mines. Miners now beginning their careers should not suffer from this disease. But for those who already have black lung, coal companies are required by federal law to pay money into a fund that goes to miners who have this disease.

There are, in fact, many ways in which the mining of coal has become a much safer occupation. All underground mines now have large fans, or ventilating systems, that keep the air circulating throughout the tunnels. These cut down on accumulations of gases. Rock-dusting and testing for gases are also required by law in underground mines. And miners must be trained in safety and first-aid methods.

A miner tests for undesirable gas levels with an electronic methane detector. In his left hand is a safety lamp, still widely used to indicate the presence of dangerous gases or shortage of oxygen.

Surface mines tend to be much safer than underground ones. Miners are, however, occasionally killed at surface mines in accidents with heavy machinery or explosives. In 1980, for instance, 22 miners were killed at surface mines, while 100 were killed in underground mines.

Today there is a federal law in the United States requiring all mines to meet certain very strict safety standards. The first law was passed in the 1950s, after a major explosion had taken place in an Illinois mine. In 1969 a new, stricter law replaced the old one. A special government group makes sure that this law is obeyed. Several times a year inspectors from the government check the mines to make sure they are safe.

5

THE COAL
MINERS

Talk to coal miners today and chances are they will tell you that their work is hard but pays well. Coal miners usually work eight hours a day, five days a week. They can, however, earn extra money by working overtime.

If you visited a coal mine, you would see that heavy machines are used to do much of the hard work involved in removing coal from the ground. People are still necessary in the mines. But now they operate machines that do the heaviest, hardest part of mining work.

There was a time, though, years ago in England and Scotland, when men, women, and even children were sent underground with picks and shovels. The women and children were used also to carry the chipped coal out of the mines in baskets. Often miners worked fourteen and fifteen hours a day, with no days off. For all that they got almost no pay. The mines were damp and unsafe then, too. The people were forced to do dangerous work in cramped, dark spaces.

Often the mine workers were under lifelong contracts to the mine owners. They virtually became slaves, with no way to escape to another job or a different way of life. These people lived miserable lives. It was a long, slow process before their situation was improved.

One major step forward occurred when laws were passed to prevent children from working in the mines. And gradually the mines were made safer, thanks to discoveries such as Sir Davy's lamp.

When mining began in the United States, many of the miners had worked in mines in Wales, Scotland, Ireland, or England. These were proud and independent people. In many communities the coal companies owned the houses where the miners lived and the stores where the miners had to buy their food and clothes. Usually the miners were not paid with money for their work. Instead they were given *script*, or paper, which could be used only for paying rent on their houses—owned, of course, by the company—or to buy goods at the stores—also owned, of course, by the company.

The miners in these communities came to resent the mine owners. They began to organize into groups and to demand better working conditions. The companies, which were rich and powerful, were able to squash most of these attempts. But the miners had one advantage: without them the coal would not be mined. So there were strikes, when the miners refused to work. And often violence between mine owners and mine workers occurred.

Finally, in the late 1800s, the miners and owners met to agree upon certain wages and conditions. This was the beginning of a strong mining union. (A union is a group of workers who organize to protect and further the interests of the union's members.) But it was still years before some companies would hire miners who belonged to the union.

One of the bloodiest battles between the union miners and the mine owners took place in 1913 in Ludlow, Colorado. The coal miners in this area had gone on strike for a pay increase. They also wanted to get the mine owners to recognize their union. The mine owners forced the miners from their homes—homes owned by the company—and in reaction the miners set up tents nearby for themselves and their families to live in. As the strike continued, the mine owners brought in troops. Shots were fired on both sides. In the fighting three men, two women, and eleven children were killed.

The mine at Ludlow was not unionized. But through the courage and efforts of many miners throughout the country, the United Mine Workers of America became, in time, a strong and accepted union. The miners were lucky to have several powerful leaders in those early days. One of them was Mother Jones, an elderly woman who believed in the miners' cause. She went from coal town to coal town, supporting and encouraging the miners in their efforts to unionize.

The most powerful and popular of all mining union leaders was John L. Lewis, president of the United Mine Workers of America from 1920 to 1960. He was a dramatic speaker and a skillful organizer. Under his leadership the miners were able to bargain for higher pay, improved safety procedures, and better conditions in the mines. Lewis also set up a fund to provide medical care for miners and their families and pensions for retired miners. Today mine owners pay into this fund more than a dollar for every ton of coal mined at their mines.

In the 1950s many home owners and industries switched from

burning coal to using gas and oil. As a result many miners were put out of work. About this time, new machines introduced into the mines made it possible to mine coal with fewer people than had been needed before. Thus mining communities grew very poor and were burdened by large numbers of unemployed. Gradually, as the electric utilities began to buy more coal, these towns grew prosperous again.

Today most coal is sold under long-term contracts, often contracts that ensure as much as thirty years' worth of work for miners. Miners can now look forward to steadier, better-paid employment. As new mines open there will be a need for thousands of new miners.

There was a time when many mining parents did not want their children to go into the mines. Now many of these miners' grandchildren are returning to the mines. New machines, good pay, and better conditions have turned coal mining into a challenging and skilled profession.

In the 1950s most of the coal mined in this country was mined by people who belonged to the United Mine Workers of America. Today only about 40 percent is mined by members of this union. Other unions, such as the United Brotherhood of Operating Engineers, have grown in membership, especially at surface mines in the western states.

Other things have changed in the mines too. Once women were considered bad luck in the mines. Now more than two thousand women are coal miners.

CLEANING AND MOVING COAL

When customers buy coal from a mine, they tell the coal company how they want their coal cleaned and sized. An electric utility company will often buy coal that has been crushed but not cleaned. Steel companies, on the other hand, need coal that has been cleaned and sorted according to size. Factories that use coal for heating are not very interested in size. But they often require that the coal be sprayed with oil, to cut down on the dust produced when the coal is unloaded.

Coal coming from a mine mixed with dirt and rock is known as **raw coal**. Electric utilities often buy this kind for their boilers. Other coal is crushed into smaller pieces. It then goes to a building near the mine known as a **preparation plant**, or **tipple**.

At the preparation plant the coal is washed in giant vats. Chemicals are added to the water in the vats so that the coal pieces float, while the dirt and rocks sink to the bottom. Next the coal is put on top of vibrating screens that sort the coal. These

A modern coal preparation plant. These plants were
once called tipples because they were buildings into
which the coal from the mine was "tipped."

Inside the plant the crushed and washed coal
is drained on a vibrating screen.

screens have holes of different sizes that allow the coal to fall through. The smaller lumps drop through the smaller holes and the very large ones stay on top.

Now the coal is ready to be moved to the market. This is a huge transportation job, since coal is so bulky.

Years ago horses and mules were used to drag coal in wagons from the mine to the customer. Later, both England and the United States developed a network of canals (artificial waterways) that served as a highway system for the boats that carried goods from one place to another. Coal was one of the major products transported on the canals.

Some coal was also moved by river barges. But the rivers were often clogged by ice in the winter and too shallow in summer. So mining took place only in the spring and fall.

Today coal is moved much faster and more efficiently, mostly because of the railroads. Trains move more than two-thirds of all the coal mined in the United States. In fact, trains move more coal than any other product.

Often a mine and the customer to whom it is selling the coal will arrange to hire a special group of rail cars, known as a **unit train**. Unit trains are usually made up of a hundred or more open-topped cars. They haul nothing but coal, and they run between the mine and the customer, with no stops in between. Often the train does not even stop to be loaded. It picks up the coal as it moves slowly under a chute at the preparation plant.

River barges are still sometimes used for moving coal. There are a few mines located right on riverbanks. In these cases the coal goes from the mine to the barge. But usually the coal is moved first by truck or train. Then it completes its journey by barge.

Unit trains help reduce the cost of moving coal.

Larger ships, called *colliers*, are used to send coal from the United States to other countries. On the Great Lakes, large freighters carry coal to Canada. Even larger vessels can carry up to 100,000 tons of coal to ports in Europe, Japan, and South America. Most coal that is sent out of the country is shipped from ports on the East Coast and the Gulf of Mexico. Ports on the West Coast are just now beginning to handle large shipments of coal.

All these methods of moving coal—by rail, by barge, and by collier—are expensive. Some mines are now experimenting with a cheaper method—moving coal through a pipeline. The coal is first crushed into small pieces and then mixed with water. This forms a thick, soupy mixture called *slurry*. The mixture is then pumped through the pipeline to the customer, where it is dried out and burned in the boilers.

There was only one coal slurry pipeline in existence in 1980. This pipeline, the Black Mesa line, runs almost 300 miles (480 km) from a mine in Arizona to an electric power plant in Nevada. More pipelines are planned and will probably be built once companies can gain permission to buy the land needed for the pipelines.

Sometimes coal does not have to be moved at all. If an area has large supplies of coal that can be mined and there is enough

Coal is loaded onto a waiting barge on the Ohio River. Barges move about ten percent of all coal mined in the United States.

water nearby, a utility plant may be built right at the mine. This eliminates the need and expense of moving the coal. Plants of this kind are called **mine-mouth plants.**

When coal people talk about coal prices, they talk about buying coal "free on board" at the mine. This means that the price does not include the cost of moving the coal. But, of course, the cost of transporting coal is important. It can add a good deal to the price of coal. This is especially true in the case of coal mined in the western states but used in the Middle West. So sometimes the price of coal seems cheap when first given. But it becomes more expensive by the time it actually reaches the customer. That is why it is to the customer's advantage to be close to the coal mine.

7

HOW WE USE COAL TODAY

If you had been around in the 1920s, your home would probably have been heated by coal. A truck would have come around every few weeks during the winter to fill up your coal bin. Today it would be unusual for you to have any coal in your home. Chances are your home is heated by gas or oil. But coal still comes into many homes in the form of electricity. More than half the electricity in our country comes from burning coal.

More than two-thirds of the coal mined in the United States is sent to electric utility plants. There it is crushed into a powder, mixed with air, and blown into a boiler, where it catches fire. The fire then heats up large tanks of water. The steam from the heated water turns giant turbines. These turbines produce the power we know as electricity.

Without electricity we would have no electric lights, no televisions, no radios, no refrigerators, no air conditioners, no garbage disposals—none of the varied conveniences many people have

come to rely on. So you can see that without coal our lives would be very different.

Natural gas and oil are also used for boilers in electric utility plants. Some people feel we should use only coal and save gas and oil for heating homes and for making gasoline.

Large amounts of coal are also used to make steel. A certain kind of bituminous coal, known as **metallurgical coal**, can be baked to make coke. Coke is coal that has had the tar and gases removed from it. It is used to heat to a very high temperature a mixture of iron ore and limestone. When the iron melts, it is purified by chemicals in the limestone and in the coke. The iron can then be used to make steel. Steel is used to make automobiles, buildings, airplanes, and trains, among other things.

The steel industry and the electric utilities together use more than three-fourths of all the coal burned each year in the United States. But coal is important to other industries as well. Cement factories, for instance, use powdered coal to heat the kilns in which cement is baked. Other factories, such as paper mills, use coal for heat and power.

Not all coal that is mined in the United States is used here. Other countries, such as Japan, France, Italy, England, and others,

Coke, a coal by-product, is pushed out of a coke oven into a quenching car before it is used in the steel-making process.

A coal stockpile in front of a coal-burning
utility plant. More than half the electricity
in the United States comes from such plants.

need coal to help provide fuel for their industries and electric utility plants. In recent years, more and more U.S. coal has been shipped abroad, or exported, for use by other countries. In 1980 about one tenth of the coal mined in the United States was exported.

Many of these countries must depend on oil from middle eastern countries for fuel for their electric utility plants. When this oil becomes too expensive, or they cannot get it because the countries it comes from are at war, they turn to coal. Coal has remained inexpensive and available. The United States, as well as Australia, South Africa and other countries, help supply coal to these countries.

In order to ship coal overseas it is necessary to have ports that are deep enough for the large ships that carry the coal across the oceans. Many ports in the United States are not deep enough for this job. In order to keep on exporting coal, the floor of many harbors must be dug out, or dredged, to make them deep enough to handle these big ships. New ports are being built now, and some ports already built will be made bigger to take care of this growing need for coal.

Once coal has been burned, you might think that it has served its usefulness. But many products can be made from the tars and gases left after coal is burned. Once coal was used to make **by-products** such as fertilizers, plastics, synthetic rubber, medicines, and hundreds of other things. Today, most of these by-products are made from oil, not coal. But if we ever need to turn to coal for this use again, it is possible to do so.

So you can be certain that even though you may not see coal anymore, it is at work for you, behind the scenes, helping to make your life easier.

COAL AND
THE ENVIRONMENT

Seven hundred years ago the king of England declared that anyone caught burning coal would be put to death. This was because the smell of coal smoke was both unpleasant and unhealthy. Much has changed since then. Today we consider burning coal a necessary part of our effort to supply enough energy for everyone. But we still have some of the same problems with the gases given off when coal is burned.

You remember that coal was formed millions of years ago from the remains of living plants. Along with the element carbon, there were other elements, such as sulfur, that stayed in the coal as it was formed. When we burn coal, this ancient sulfur is released into the air in the form of a gas known as **sulfur dioxide**. Scientists have learned that too much sulfur dioxide in the air can harm people's lungs and can make breathing difficult. It can also have a damaging effect on trees and plants. **Nitrogen dioxide** is also released when coal is burned. It can cause rain and snow to have a higher than normal acid content.

Coal also contains a certain amount of ash. Unless the ash is removed from the smokestacks in factories heated by coal, the air in the area will become filled with soot and grime. Fortunately, scientists have developed equipment that will take the ash out of coal smoke. These devices act like very strong magnets. They collect the particles that fly into the air as coal is burned. Almost all places that burn large amounts of coal are equipped with these collectors. Nowadays there is no reason for people to put up with dirty air just because they live in an area where coal is burned.

In order to keep our air as healthy as possible, the United States Congress passed a law called the Clean Air Act. This law says that any company that burns coal must have some method of controlling the sulfur dioxide that results when coal is burned. Scientists also have developed equipment called *scrubbers*, which remove much of the sulfur dioxide by passing the coal through a water and limestone spray. But these scrubbers are very expensive to build and use. The extra money needed to operate these scrubbers means that customers pay more for their electricity.

Another method of keeping sulfur out of the air is to burn coal that does not have much sulfur in it. As a result, low-sulfur coal is very much in demand by the many electric companies. These companies burn large quantities of coal. But to meet state and national standards, they must limit the amounts of sulfur dioxide that can be released into the air.

A third way of controlling sulfur dioxide is to burn coal in a *fluidized bed*, or on a vibrating screen, where the burning coal is mixed with air and powdered limestone.

Grain grows on a reclaimed strip mine while
active mining goes on in the background.

Methods for controlling nitrogen dioxide are still being examined.

Air pollution is only one of the environmental concerns about coal. Many people in the United States were upset because of the way the land was left after coal companies surface-mined for coal. In the past, land was often left bare and unattractive once the coal had been removed. Over the years, state governments began to require that coal companies plant the land, or reclaim it, once they had mined it. In 1977 the United States Congress passed a national law that said that all land that was strip mined for coal would have to be reclaimed according to very strict standards.

Today, a company that mines coal at a surface mine must make sure that the land is returned to just as good or better shape than before it was mined. To do this the companies must grade the land, or smooth it out with bulldozers. Then they must find plants or trees that will grow in the climate in that area, fertilize the land, and plant and tend the vegetation. The companies must also protect the animals in the area before, during, and after the mining.

For the land that was mined many years ago and never reclaimed, coal companies must now pay a certain amount for every ton of coal they mine. The money goes into a special fund that is used to reclaim this old, barren land.

To make sure that they obey the law and to find better ways to reclaim land, most coal companies now employ special mining engineers, water and plant experts, and other environmental specialists.

COAL IN
THE FUTURE

In the past, coal has always been burned in a solid form. But in the years to come, coal will be used in new ways and will even be changed into gas and oil. When coal is changed into gas or oil, the new product is called a **synthetic fuel**.

For many years now, scientists have been experimenting with coal in laboratories. They have discovered that the elements that make up a lump of coal are the same as those elements found in gas and oil.

You remember that coal is made up mostly of carbon, with some hydrogen. So are gas and oil. But both gas and oil have more hydrogen than coal does. In coal there is about one part carbon to one part hydrogen. Oil has about one part carbon to two parts hydrogen. Gas is the richest in hydrogen; it has about one part carbon to four parts hydrogen.

To change coal to oil or gas, researchers have found a way to add more hydrogen to coal. The coal is crushed and heated, under pressure, to a very high temperature. Then a stream of air, which contains hydrogen, is blown across the gases given off by the coal when it is burned. The gases then turn into either gas or oil, depending on how much hydrogen is present.

At this time, changing coal into gas and oil is still quite expensive. Engineers are exploring ways to bring the costs down. The aim is to make it possible for us to afford gasoline made from coal for our automobiles and gas made from coal for heating our homes.

Some researchers are experimenting with turning coal into gas before the coal is removed from the ground. To do this, air is piped underground to the coal seams. The coal begins to burn. The gases then given off by the burning coal rise to the surface, where they are purified and sent to markets through pipes.

The advantage of changing coal into gas or oil is that the sulfur is removed from the fuel in the process. Thus it can burn without polluting the air. Also, gas and oil are easier to transport than coal. However, making synthetic fuels from coal may damage the environment, and researchers are looking for ways to control these harmful effects.

In still other experiments, coal experts are working with new ways to make electricity from coal. One method they are working on, called a fuel cell, involves heating coal to a high temperature and then passing the gases from it through a magnetic field. As the particles in the gases cut the magnetic field, they produce electricity. This process is still in the experimental stages. But if it succeeds, it will mean less coal can be used than is now used in our electric utility plants.

Not all the research in the coal industry is directed toward how to use coal. There are also many people working to find better ways

of getting the coal out of the ground. In surface mining, company officials are working on ways to remove the overburden and the coal so that the reclamation can be done more quickly and more successfully. In underground mining, researchers are finding methods to make mining safer and to improve methods of removing and moving the coal. Some companies are now using computers to make coal mining more efficient. Others are experimenting with laser beams for tunneling and mining underground.

The work that coal researchers are doing today will determine in part how we live tomorrow. The importance of coal goes back hundreds of years. Blood has been spilled over it, societies have been changed because of it, and people have suffered—and prospered—because of it. But coal will be with us for hundreds of years more. Our challenges now are to develop new ways to mine coal and to learn how to use it wisely in the future.

For the future. This large-scale test plant experiments with turning coal into natural gas.

GLOSSARY OF IMPORTANT WORDS

Anthracite. Carbon-rich hard coal which, when it burns, gives off much heat and little smoke.

Bituminous coal. Soft coal which, when it burns, gives off a little less heat and a little more smoke than anthracite.

Black lung. A disease gotten by inhaling too much coal dust. Black lung causes shortness of breath and may cause death.

By-products. Gases and chemicals gotten from coal *after* it is burned. These by-products are used in manufacturing other products, such as medicines, insect sprays, and plastics.

Carboniferous Period. The time period when coal was formed on the earth from ancient vegetation. Also called the *Coal Age.*

Coal Age. *See* Carboniferous Period.

Coal face. The section of the exposed coal bed that the miners work on.

Coal outcrop. An area where the coal comes to the surface. Coal outcrops help miners locate coal deposits.

Coke. Coal from which most of the gases have been removed by heating. Coke is used extensively in the making of steel from iron ore.

Drift mine. A type of underground mine set up where coal is exposed on a hillside. A horizontal tunnel is dug through to the coal bed.

Land reclamation. The process of renewing strip-mined land for some useful purpose.

Lignite. A soft brown coal, softer than sub-bituminous coal but harder than peat.

Metallurgical coal. A kind of bituminous coal used for the baking of coke.

Methane monitor. A device that measures the amount of methane gas in an underground mine. Methane gas, when mixed with air in a certain proportion, can cause an explosion.

Mine-mouth plants. Utility plants set up near coal mines. This arrangement cuts down on the cost of moving the coal.

Overburden. The rock or dirt above a coal seam. The overburden is removed by electric shovels or excavators in surface mining.

Peat. A mass of ancient compressed plants and grass found in swampy areas. It can be used as a fertilizer or dried and used as a fuel.

Preparation plant. A building near a mine where coal goes for cleaning and sizing before it is transported to customers. Also called *tipple*.

Raw coal. Coal that has not been cleaned or sized. This coal is used heavily by electric utility companies for their boilers.

Sea coal. The coal outcrop found near the North Sea in England in the thirteenth century.

Shaft mine. A type of underground mine set up when coal lies below the ground. A vertical hole is drilled and a cage is set up to take miners to the coal face.

Slope mine. A type of underground mine set up when a coal seam lies beneath a hill. A sloping tunnel is dug out to get to the coal.

Strip mining. A type of mining used where the coal bed lies close to the surface and can be removed by digging away the overburden. Also called *surface mining*.

Sub-bituminous coal. Very soft, fairly carbon-rich coal, softer than bituminous coal but harder than lignite.

Sulfur dioxide. The gas given off when coal is burned. It is unpleasant to smell and dangerous to breathe in large amounts.

Surface mining. *See* Strip mining.

Tipple. *See* Preparation plant.

Underground mining. The type of mining used when coal lies buried deep in the earth, and shafts or tunnels must be constructed to reach the coal seam.

Unit train. A series of a hundred or so rail cars that load only with coal and make nonstop runs between the mine preparation plants and one customer.

INDEX